THE BEST
STEELY DAN

Original Scores for Vocals, Solo Guitar, Solo Keyboard, Synthesizer, Keyboards, Bass, Percussion & Drums

ISBN 978-0-7935-2531-7

HAL•LEONARD®
CORPORATION

7777 W. BLUEMOUND RD. P.O. BOX 13819 MILWAUKEE, WI 53213

Visit Hal Leonard Online at
www.halleonard.com

D R U M   K E Y

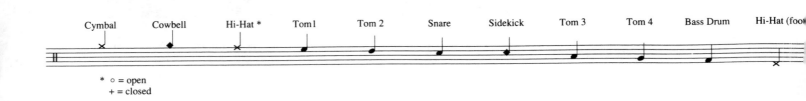

* ○ = open
  + = closed

CONTENTS

AJA

Words and Music by WALTER BECKER
and DONALD FAGEN

6

To Coda ⊕

BLACK FRIDAY

Words and Music by WALTER BECKER
and DONALD FAGEN

Repeat and Fade

DEACON BLUES

Words and Music by WALTER BECKER
and DONALD FAGEN

DO IT AGAIN

Words and Music by WALTER BECKER
and DONALD FAGEN

* Ad lib. fills during verses and on fade out.

Additional Lyrics

2. When you know she's no high climber
Then you find your only friend
In a room with your two timer
And you're sure you're near the end.

Then you love a little wild one
And she brings you only sorrow,
All the time you know she's smilin'
You'll be on your knees tomorrow.

Chorus

3. Now you swear and kick and beg us
That you're not a gamblin' man;
Then you find you're back in Vegas
With a handle in your hand.

Your black cards can make you money
So you hide them when you're able;
In the land of milk and honey
You must put them on the table.

Chorus

HEY NINETEEN

Words and Music by WALTER BECKER
and DONALD FAGEN

Repeat and Fade

KID CHARLEMAGNE

Words and Music by WALTER BECKER
and DONALD FAGEN

58

62

MY OLD SCHOOL

Words and Music by WALTER BECKER
and DONALD FAGEN

PEG

Words and Music by WALTER BECKER
and DONALD FAGEN

REELING IN THE YEARS

Words and Music by WALTER BECKER
and DONALD FAGEN

84

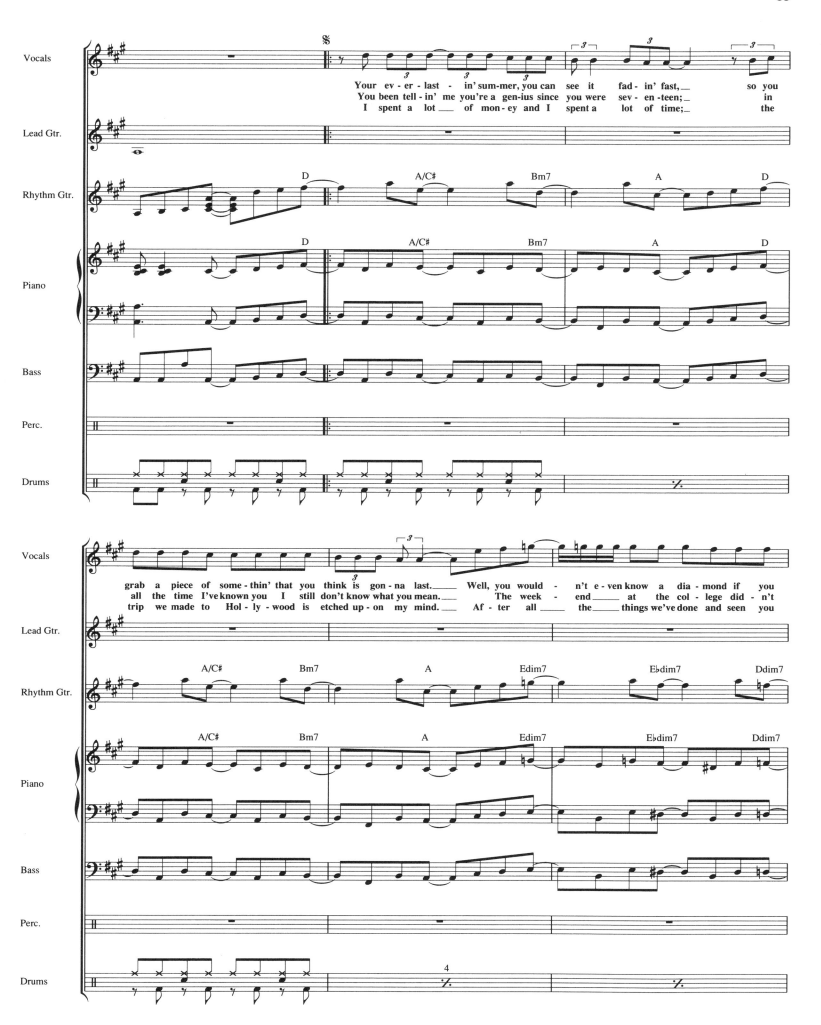

RIKKI DON'T LOSE THAT NUMBER

Words and Music by WALTER BECKER
and DONALD FAGEN

TIME OUT OF MIND

Words and Music by WALTER BECKER
and DONALD FAGEN

108

114

Transcribed SCORES®

Transcribed Scores are vocal and instrumental arrangements of music from some of the greatest groups in music. These excellent publications feature transcribed parts for lead vocals, lead guitar, rhythm, guitar, bass, drums, and all of the various instruments used in each specific recording session. All songs are arranged exactly the way the artists recorded them.

00672463	Aerosmith – Big Ones	$24.95
00672527	Audioslave	$24.95
00673228	The Beatles – Complete Scores (Boxed Set)	$79.95
00672378	The Beatles – Transcribed Scores	$24.95
00673208	Best of Blood, Sweat & Tears	$19.95
00690636	Best of Bluegrass	$24.95
00672367	Chicago – Volume 1	$24.95
00672368	Chicago – Volume 2	$24.95
00672452	Miles Davis – Birth of the Cool	$24.95
00672460	Miles Davis – Kind of Blue (Sketch Scores)	$19.95
00672490	Miles Davis – Kind of Blue (Hardcover)	$29.95
00672502	Deep Purple – Greatest Hits	$24.95
00672327	Gil Evans Collection	$24.95
00672508	Ben Folds – Rockin' the Suburbs	$19.95
00672427	Ben Folds Five – Selections from Naked Baby Photos	$19.95
00672458	Ben Folds Five – The Unauthorized Biography of Reinhold Messner	$19.95
00672428	Ben Folds Five – Whatever and Ever, Amen	$19.95
00672399	Foo Fighters	$24.95
00672517	Foo Fighters – One by One	$24.95
00672472	Goo Goo Dolls Collection	$24.95
00672540	Best of Good Charlotte	$24.95
00672396	The Don Grolnick Collection	$17.95
00672308	Jimi Hendrix – Are You Experienced?	$29.95
00672345	Jimi Hendrix – Axis Bold As Love	$29.95
00672313	Jimi Hendrix – Band of Gypsys	$29.95
00672397	Jimi Hendrix – Experience Hendrix	$29.95
00672500	Best of Incubus	$24.95
00672469	Billy Joel Collection	$24.95
00672415	Eric Johnson – Ah Via Musicom	$24.95
00672499	John Lennon – Greatest Hits	$24.95
00672465	John Lennon – Imagine	$24.95

00672478	The Best of Megadeth	$24.95
00672504	Gary Moore – Greatest Hits	$24.95
00690582	Nickel Creek – Nickel Creek	$19.95
00690586	Nickel Creek – This Side	$19.95
00672518	Nirvana	$24.95
00672424	Nirvana – Bleach	$24.95
00672403	Nirvana – In Utero	$24.95
00672404	Nirvana – Incesticide	$24.95
00672402	Nirvana – Nevermind	$24.95
00672405	Nirvana – Unplugged in New York	$24.95
00672466	The Offspring – Americana	$24.95
00672501	The Police – Greatest Hits	$24.95
00672538	The Best of Queen	$24.95
00672400	Red Hot Chili Peppers – Blood Sugar Sex Magik	$24.95
00672515	Red Hot Chili Peppers – By the Way	$24.95
00672456	Red Hot Chili Peppers – Californication	$24.95
00672536	Red Hot Chili Peppers – Greatest Hits	$24.95
00672422	Red Hot Chili Peppers – Mother's Milk	$24.95
00672551	Red Hot Chili Peppers – Stadium Arcadium	$49.95
00672408	Rolling Stones – Exile on Main Street	$24.95
00672360	Santana's Greatest Hits	$26.95
00672522	The Best of Slipknot	$24.95
00675170	The Best of Spyro Gyra	$18.95
00675200	The Best of Steely Dan	$19.95
00672468	Sting – Fields of Gold	$24.95
00674655	Sting – Nothing Like the Sun	$19.95
00673230	Sting – Ten Summoner's Tales	$19.95
00672521	Best of SUM 41	$29.95
00675520	Best of Weather Report	$18.95

Prices and availability subject to change

0308

NOTE-FOR-NOTE KEYBOARD TRANSCRIPTIONS

These outstanding collections feature note-for-note transcriptions from the artists who made the songs famous. No matter what style you play, these books are perfect for performers or students who want to play just like their keyboard idols.

ACOUSTIC PIANO BALLADS

16 acoustic piano favorites: Angel • Candle in the Wind • Don't Let the Sun Go Down on Me • Endless Love • Imagine • It's Too Late • Let It Be • Mandy • Ribbon in the Sky • Sailing • She's Got a Way • So Far Away • Tapestry • You Never Give Me Your Money • You've Got a Friend • Your Song.

00690351 / $19.95

ELTON JOHN

18 of Elton John's best songs: Bennie and the Jets • Candle in the Wind • Crocodile Rock • Daniel • Don't Let the Sun Go Down on Me • Goodbye Yellow Brick Road • I Guess That's Why They Call It the Blues • Little Jeannie • Rocket Man • Your Song • and more!

00694829 / $20.95

THE BEATLES KEYBOARD BOOK

23 Beatles favorites, including: All You Need Is Love • Back in the U.S.S.R. • Come Together • Get Back • Good Day Sunshine • Hey Jude • Lady Madonna • Let It Be • Lucy in the Sky with Diamonds • Ob-La-Di, Ob-La-Da • Oh! Darling • Penny Lane • Revolution • We Can Work It Out • With a Little Help from My Friends • and more.

00694827 / $20.95

THE CAROLE KING KEYBOARD BOOK

16 of King's greatest songs: Beautiful • Been to Canaan • Home Again • I Feel the Earth Move • It's Too Late • Jazzman • (You Make Me Feel) Like a Natural Woman • Nightingale • Smackwater Jack • So Far Away • Sweet Seasons • Tapestry • Way Over Yonder • Where You Lead • Will You Love Me Tomorrow • You've Got a Friend.

00690554 / $19.95

CLASSIC ROCK

35 all-time rock classics: Beth • Bloody Well Right • Changes • Cold as Ice • Come Sail Away • Don't Do Me like That • Hard to Handle • Heaven • Killer Queen • King of Pain • Layla • Light My Fire • Oye Como Va • Piano Man • Takin' Care of Business • Werewolves of London • and more.

00310940 / $24.95

POP/ROCK

35 songs, including: Africa • Against All Odds • Axel F • Centerfold • Chariots of Fire • Cherish • Don't Let the Sun Go Down on Me • Drops of Jupiter (Tell Me) • Faithfully • It's Too Late • Just the Way You Are • Let It Be • Mandy • Sailing • Sweet Dreams Are Made of This • Walking in Memphis • and more.

00310939 / $24.95

JAZZ

24 favorites from Bill Evans, Thelonious Monk, Oscar Peterson, Bud Powell, Art Tatum and more. Includes: Ain't Misbehavin' • April in Paris • Autumn in New York • Body and Soul • Freddie Freeloader • Giant Steps • My Funny Valentine • Satin Doll • Song for My Father • Stella by Starlight • and more.

00310941 / $22.95

R&B

35 R&B classics: Baby Love • Boogie on Reggae Woman • Easy • Endless Love • Fallin' • Green Onions • Higher Ground • I'll Be There • Just Once • Money (That's What I Want) • On the Wings of Love • Ribbon in the Sky • This Masquerade • Three Times a Lady • and more.

00310942 / $24.95

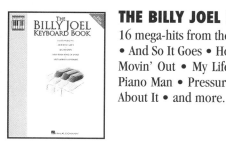

THE BILLY JOEL KEYBOARD BOOK

16 mega-hits from the Piano Man himself: Allentown • And So It Goes • Honesty • Just the Way You Are • Movin' Out • My Life • New York State of Mind • Piano Man • Pressure • She's Got a Way • Tell Her About It • and more.

00694828 / $22.95

STEVIE WONDER

14 of Stevie's most popular songs: Boogie on Reggae Woman • Hey Love • Higher Ground • I Wish • Isn't She Lovely • Lately • Living for the City • Overjoyed • Ribbon in the Sky • Send One Your Love • Superstition • That Girl • You Are the Sunshine of My Life • You Haven't Done Nothin'.

00306698 / $21.95

Prices, contents and availability subject to change without notice.

FOR MORE INFORMATION, SEE YOUR LOCAL MUSIC DEALER,
OR WRITE TO:

HAL•LEONARD®
CORPORATION
7777 W. BLUEMOUND RD. P.O. BOX 13819 MILWAUKEE, WI 53213

Visit Hal Leonard online at www.halleonard.com

0107

RECORDED VERSIONS®
The Best Note-For-Note Transcriptions Available

RECORDED VERSIONS GUITAR

ALL BOOKS INCLUDE TABLATURE

00692015	Aerosmith – Greatest Hits	$22.95
00690603	Aerosmith – O Yeah! (Ultimate Hits)	$24.95
00690178	Alice in Chains – Acoustic	$19.95
00694865	Alice in Chains – Dirt	$19.95
00690387	Alice in Chains – Nothing Safe: The Best of the Box	$19.95
00690812	All American Rejects – Move Along	$19.95
00694932	Allman Brothers Band – Volume 1	$24.95
00694933	Allman Brothers Band – Volume 2	$24.95
00694934	Allman Brothers Band – Volume 3	$24.95
00690865	Atreyu – A Deathgrip on Yesterday	$19.95
00690609	Audioslave	$19.95
00690804	Audioslave – Out of Exile	$19.95
00690884	Audioslave – Revelations	$19.95
00690820	Avenged Sevenfold – City of Evil	$22.95
00690366	Bad Company – Original Anthology, Book 1	$19.95
00690503	Beach Boys – Very Best of	$19.95
00690489	Beatles – 1	$24.95
00694929	Beatles – 1962-1966	$24.95
00694930	Beatles – 1967-1970	$24.95
00694832	Beatles – For Acoustic Guitar	$22.95
00690110	Beatles – White Album (Book 1)	$19.95
00692385	Chuck Berry	$19.95
00690835	Billy Talent	$19.95
00692200	Black Sabbath – We Sold Our Soul for Rock 'N' Roll	$19.95
00690674	blink-182	$19.95
00690831	blink-182 – Greatest Hits	$19.95
00690491	David Bowie – Best of	$19.95
00690873	Breaking Benjamin – Phobia	$19.95
00690764	Breaking Benjamin – We Are Not Alone	$19.95
00690451	Jeff Buckley – Collection	$24.95
00690590	Eric Clapton – Anthology	$29.95
00690415	Clapton Chronicles – Best of Eric Clapton	$18.95
00690074	Eric Clapton – The Cream of Clapton	$24.95
00690716	Eric Clapton – Me and Mr. Johnson	$19.95
00694869	Eric Clapton – Unplugged	$22.95
00690162	The Clash – Best of	$19.95
00690828	Coheed & Cambria – Good Apollo I'm Burning Star, IV, Vol. 1: From Fear Through the Eyes of Madness	$19.95
00690593	Coldplay – A Rush of Blood to the Head	$19.95
00690838	Cream – Royal Albert Hall: London May 2-3-5-6 2005	$22.95
00690856	Creed – Greatest Hits	$22.95
00690401	Creed – Human Clay	$19.95
00690819	Creedence Clearwater Revival – Best of	$19.95
00690572	Steve Cropper – Soul Man	$19.95
00690613	Crosby, Stills & Nash – Best of	$19.95
00690289	Deep Purple – Best of	$17.95
00690784	Def Leppard – Best of	$19.95
00690347	The Doors – Anthology	$22.95
00690348	The Doors – Essential Guitar Collection	$16.95
00690810	Fall Out Boy – From Under the Cork Tree	$19.95
00690664	Fleetwood Mac – Best of	$19.95
00690870	Flyleaf	$19.95
00690808	Foo Fighters – In Your Honor	$19.95
00690805	Robben Ford – Best of	$19.95
00694920	Free – Best of	$19.95
00690848	Godsmack – IV	$19.95
00690601	Good Charlotte – The Young and the Hopeless	$19.95
00690697	Jim Hall – Best of	$19.95
00690840	Ben Harper – Both Sides of the Gun	$19.95
00694798	George Harrison – Anthology	$19.95
00692930	Jimi Hendrix – Are You Experienced?	$24.95

00692931	Jimi Hendrix – Axis: Bold As Love	$22.95
00690608	Jimi Hendrix – Blue Wild Angel	$24.95
00692932	Jimi Hendrix – Electric Ladyland	$24.95
00690017	Jimi Hendrix – Live at Woodstock	$24.95
00690602	Jimi Hendrix – Smash Hits	$19.95
00690843	H.I.M. – Dark Light	$19.95
00690869	Hinder – Extreme Behavior	$19.95
00690692	Billy Idol – Very Best of	$19.95
00690688	Incubus – A Crow Left of the Murder	$19.95
00690457	Incubus – Make Yourself	$19.95
00690544	Incubus – Morningview	$19.95
00690790	Iron Maiden Anthology	$24.95
00690730	Alan Jackson – Guitar Collection	$19.95
00690721	Jet – Get Born	$19.95
00690684	Jethro Tull – Aqualung	$19.95
00690647	Jewel – Best of	$19.95
00690814	John5 – Songs for Sanity	$19.95
00690751	John5 – Vertigo	$19.95
00690845	Eric Johnson – Bloom	$19.95
00690846	Jack Johnson and Friends – Sing-A-Longs and Lullabies for the Film Curious George	$19.95
00690271	Robert Johnson – New Transcriptions	$24.95
00699131	Janis Joplin – Best of	$19.95
00690427	Judas Priest – Best of	$19.95
00690742	The Killers – Hot Fuss	$19.95
00694903	Kiss – Best of	$24.95
00690780	Korn – Greatest Hits, Volume 1	$22.95
00690834	Lamb of God – Ashes of the Wake	$19.95
00690875	Lamb of God – Sacrament	$19.95
00690823	Ray LaMontagne – Trouble	$19.95
00690679	John Lennon – Guitar Collection	$19.95
00690781	Linkin Park – Hybrid Theory	$22.95
00690782	Linkin Park – Meteora	$22.95
00690783	Live – Best of	$19.95
00690743	Los Lonely Boys	$19.95
00690876	Los Lonely Boys – Sacred	$19.95
00690720	Lostprophets – Start Something	$19.95
00694954	Lynyrd Skynyrd – New Best of	$19.95
00690752	Lynyrd Skynyrd – Street Survivors	$19.95
00690577	Yngwie Malmsteen – Anthology	$24.95
00690754	Marilyn Manson – Lest We Forget	$19.95
00694956	Bob Marley – Legend	$19.95
00694945	Bob Marley – Songs of Freedom	$24.95
00690657	Maroon5 – Songs About Jane	$19.95
00120080	Don McLean – Songbook	$19.95
00694951	Megadeth – Rust in Peace	$22.95
00690768	Megadeth – The System Has Failed	$19.95
00690505	John Mellencamp – Guitar Collection	$19.95
00690646	Pat Metheny – One Quiet Night	$19.95
00690558	Pat Metheny – Trio: 99>00	$19.95
00690040	Steve Miller Band – Young Hearts	$19.95
00690794	Mudvayne – Lost and Found	$19.95
00690611	Nirvana	$22.95
00694883	Nirvana – Nevermind	$19.95
00690026	Nirvana – Unplugged in New York	$19.95
00690807	The Offspring – Greatest Hits	$19.95
00694847	Ozzy Osbourne – Best of	$22.95
00690399	Ozzy Osbourne – Ozzman Cometh	$19.95
00690866	Panic! At the Disco – A Fever You Can't Sweat Out	$19.95
00694855	Pearl Jam – Ten	$19.95
00690439	A Perfect Circle – Mer De Noms	$19.95
00690661	A Perfect Circle – Thirteenth Step	$19.95
00690499	Tom Petty – Definitive Guitar Collection	$19.95
00690428	Pink Floyd – Dark Side of the Moon	$19.95
00690789	Poison – Best of	$19.95
00693864	The Police – Best of	$19.95

00694975	Queen – Greatest Hits	$24.
00690670	Queensryche – Very Best of	$19.
00690878	The Raconteurs – Broken Boy Soldiers	$19.
00694910	Rage Against the Machine	$19.
00690055	Red Hot Chili Peppers – Blood Sugar Sex Magik	$19.
00690584	Red Hot Chili Peppers – By the Way	$19.
00690379	Red Hot Chili Peppers – Californication	$19.
00690673	Red Hot Chili Peppers – Greatest Hits	$19.
00690852	Red Hot Chili Peppers – Stadium Arcadium	$24.
00690511	Django Reinhardt – Definitive Collection	$19.
00690779	Relient K – MMHMM	$19.
00690643	Relient K – Two Lefts Don't Make a Right...But Three Do	$19.
00690631	Rolling Stones – Guitar Anthology	$24.
00690685	David Lee Roth – Eat 'Em and Smile	$19.
00690694	David Lee Roth – Guitar Anthology	$24.
00690031	Santana's Greatest Hits	$19.
00690796	Michael Schenker – Very Best of	$19.
00690566	Scorpions – Best of	$19.
00690604	Bob Seger – Guitar Collection	$19.
00690803	Kenny Wayne Shepherd Band – Best of	$19.
00690857	Shinedown – Us and Them	$19.
00690530	Slipknot – Iowa	$19.
00690733	Slipknot – Vol. 3 (The Subliminal Verses)	$19.
00120004	Steely Dan – Best of	$24.
00694921	Steppenwolf – Best of	$22.
00690655	Mike Stern – Best of	$19.
00690877	Stone Sour – Come What(ever) May	$19.
00690520	Styx Guitar Collection	$19.
00120081	Sublime	$19.
00690771	SUM 41 – Chuck	$19.
00690767	Switchfoot – The Beautiful Letdown	$19.
00690830	System of a Down – Hypnotize	$19.
00690799	System of a Down – Mezmerize	$19.
00690531	System of a Down – Toxicity	$19.
00694824	James Taylor – Best of	$16.
00690871	Three Days Grace – One-X	$19.
00690737	3 Doors Down – The Better Life	$22
00690683	Robin Trower – Bridge of Sighs	$19.
00690740	Shania Twain – Guitar Collection	$19
00699191	U2 – Best of: 1980-1990	$19.
00690732	U2 – Best of: 1990-2000	$19.
00690575	U2 – How to Dismantle an Atomic Bomb	$22
00690575	Steve Vai – Alive in an Ultra World	$22.
00660137	Steve Vai – Passion & Warfare	$24.
00690116	Stevie Ray Vaughan – Guitar Collection	$24.
00660058	Stevie Ray Vaughan – Lightnin' Blues 1983-1987	$24.
00694835	Stevie Ray Vaughan – The Sky Is Crying	$22.
00690015	Stevie Ray Vaughan – Texas Flood	$19.
00690772	Velvet Revolver – Contraband	$22.
00690071	Weezer (The Blue Album)	$19
00690447	The Who – Best of	$24.
00690589	ZZ Top Guitar Anthology	$22

Bass Recorded Versions® feature authentic transcriptions written in standard notation and tablature for bass guitar. This series features complete bass lines from the classics to contemporary superstars.

25 All-Time Rock Bass Classics
00690445 / $14.95

25 Essential Rock Bass Classics
00690210 / $15.95

Aerosmith Bass Collection
00690413 / $17.95

Best of Victor Bailey
00690718 / $19.95

Bass Tab 1990-1999
00690400 / $16.95

Bass Tab 1999-2000
00690404 / $14.95

Bass Tab White Pages
00690508 / $29.95

The Beatles Bass Lines
00690170 / $14.95

The Beatles 1962-1966
00690556 / $17.95

The Beatles 1967-1970
00690557 / $16.95

Best Bass Rock Hits
00694803 / $12.95

**Black Sabbath –
We Sold Our Soul For Rock 'N' Roll**
00660116 / $17.95

The Best of Blink 182
00690549 / $18.95

Blues Bass Classics
00690291 / $14.95

Chart Hits for Bass
00690729 / $14.95

The Best of Eric Clapton
00660187 / $19.95

Stanley Clarke Collection
00672307 / $19.95

Funk Bass Bible
00690744 / $19.95

Hard Rock Bass Bible
00690746 / $17.95

**Jimi Hendrix –
Are You Experienced?**
00690371 / $17.95

The Buddy Holly Bass Book
00660132 / $12.95

Incubus – Morning View
00690639 / $17.95

Best of Kiss for Bass
00690080 / $19.95

Bob Marley Bass Collection
00690568 / $19.95

Best of Marcus Miller
00690811 / $19.95

Motown Bass Classics
00690253 / $14.95

Mudvayne – Lost & Found
00690798 / $19.95

Nirvana Bass Collection
00690066 / $19.95

No Doubt – Tragic Kingdom
00120112 / $22.95

The Offspring – Greatest Hits
00690809 / $17.95

**Jaco Pastorius –
Greatest Jazz Fusion Bass Player**
00690421 / $17.95

The Essential Jaco Pastorius
00690420 / $18.95

Pearl Jam – Ten
00694882 / $14.95

Pink Floyd – Dark Side of the Moon
00660172 / $14.95

The Best of Police
00660207 / $14.95

Pop/Rock Bass Bible
00690747 / $17.95

Queen – The Bass Collection
00690065 / $17.95

R&B Bass Bible
00690745 / $17.95

Rage Against the Machine
00690248 / $16.95

The Best of Red Hot Chili Peppers
00695285 / $24.95

**Red Hot Chili Peppers –
Blood Sugar Sex Magik**
00690064 / $19.95

**Red Hot Chili Peppers –
By the Way**
00690585 / $19.95

**Red Hot Chili Peppers –
Californication**
00690390 / $19.95

**Red Hot Chili Peppers –
Greatest Hits**
00690675 / $18.95

**Red Hot Chili Peppers –
One Hot Minute**
00690091 / $18.95

Rock Bass Bible
00690446 / $19.95

Rolling Stones
00690256 / $16.95

System of a Down – Toxicity
00690592 / $19.95

Top Hits for Bass
00690677 / $14.95

**Stevie Ray Vaughan –
Lightnin' Blues 1983-1987**
00694778 / $19.95

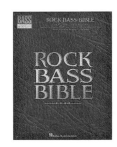

0308